Just Breathe Again!

Just Breathe Again!

He is as close as your next breath...

Kiya Cordeau
Limitless Life Publishing
2019

First Printing: 2019

All Scripture quotations are taken from the Holy Bible: New King James Version unless otherwise noted.

Scripture taken from the New King James Version®. Copyright © 1982 by Thomas Nelson. Used by permission. All rights reserved.

Scriptures taken from the Holy Bible, New International Version®, NIV®. Copyright © 1973, 1978, 1984, 2011 by Biblica, Inc.™ Used by permission of Zondervan. All rights reserved worldwide. www.zondervan.com

Scripture taken from The Message. Copyright © 1993, 1994, 1995, 1996, 2000, 2001, 2002. Used by permission of NavPress Publishing Group."

Scripture taken from The Living Bible copyright © 1971 by Tyndale House Foundation. Used by permission of Tyndale House Publishers Inc., Carol Stream, Illinois 60188. All rights reserved.

Scripture quotations marked (AMP) are taken from the Amplified Bible, Copyright © 1954, 1958, 1962, 1964, 1965, 1987 by The Lockman Foundation. Used by permission.

ISBN 978-0-578-23023-8

Published by:
Limitless Life Publishing
4611 S. University Drive
Suite 267
Davie, FL 33328

Website: www.davidcordeau.com

Cover Design by Aaron Garcia
mediagrow@yahoo.com
Facebook/Instagram: @churchmediagrow

To my mom and dad, Mary and Harold Pinckney, to whom I owe not just the inheritance of my DNA, but making Psalm 139 come alive in me from the very beginning.

> *"For you formed my inward parts; You covered me in my mother's womb. I will praise you for I am fearfully and wonderfully made; And that my soul knows very well."*
>
> *Psalm 139:13-14*

I have been crucified with Christ: and I myself no longer live, but Christ lives in me. And the real life I now have within this body is a result of my trusting in the Son of God, who loved me and gave himself for me.

Galatians 2:20 (The Living Bible)

Contents

Acknowledgments

A tremendous thank you goes to my family, my greatest blessing: David, my husband for almost 26 years and my children, Elisha, Cherie, and Jordan, who never cease to amaze me with their love, quick wit, and colorful personalities. I want to acknowledge my parents, Harold and Mary Pinckney and my in-laws, David and Nolia Cordeau who have made an incredible mark on my life through their faithfulness, perseverance, and service to God and others. They continue to be role models and pillars in our family. Thank you all for your encouragement and love. A big thank you goes to my closest friend and sister, Adrienne Ross, for writing *Push Your Way to Purpose* and pushing me to write! I am forever grateful for you.

Thank you to all my family and friends throughout the years who have taught me so much through your life and love.

A special thank you goes to a dear family friend and former pastor's wife, Bessie Lee Perry (1923-2018) ~ I fondly remember her as the faithful mother of eight and wife who taught me how to worship, when to worship, and how to seek God. As a wife of a fiery Pentecostal preacher, her melodious voice would ring out a tune written by Rev. Paul Jones on a Sunday evening that could right all wrongs...

"God has been good to me. He has been so good to me. More than this world could ever be, He has been so good to me. He drives my tears away; He turns my midnight into day. So, I'll just say thank you, Lord and I won't complain."

Most of all, thank you, Jesus, for the breath that I breathe and the words You have penned on my heart to share with others.

Introduction

After years of singing, stretching and damaging my vocal cords, I found myself working to restore my range and quality of sound. I prayed, fasted, repented, did flips in my living room, everything and anything I could think of that would bring back the melodious "gift" God had given me. Although I had some success, it wasn't until I listened to the Holy Spirit bring understanding to me through our church vocal coach that I found solid ground.

Fondly remembering a vocal lesson, I attended, Lily stopped the vocal exercise, looked at me, and in her light-hearted Colombian accent said, "Pastora, what are you doing? What's the problem?" I, of course, laughed as usual when we're together and embarrassingly responded, "I'm afraid I won't have enough air." She paused and nonchalantly threw out, "Just breathe again." After at least five minutes of medicinal laughter, I managed to say, "Oh, that's easy!" She explained that you cannot effectively sing with a full sound AND reserve air. Use the air and you will have more rather than not enough. Suddenly, revelation struck me like the finale of an orchestra performance - I could breathe again! What was the Lord telling me? He was showing me that it really was easy - simply breathe again. How many times in our lives have we faced challenges daily, weekly, monthly, yearly praying for a better day, a better turnout? God doesn't expect us to breathe in once and continue with life. He simply directs us to breathe - Breathe what? Breathe in life!

Have you ever caught yourself holding your breath? Maybe while you were talking and suddenly you realized you were holding your breath? Why? It's silly to think of. Our bodies are created to take a breath automatically, depending on our age, 12-60 times per minute; that's 17,000-30,000 breaths per day![1] Unless we purposely hold our breath, we breathe. What causes us to hold our breath? Excitement, stress, anxiety, fear, exhaustion - "waiting to exhale". It's time to *Just Breathe Again!*

---

[1] Wonderopolis.org Science, "Have You Ever Wondered…"National Center for Families Learning

Chapter One

An Encounter

Our first breath begins with the following verse:

The message is very close at hand; it is on your lips
and in your heart. And that message is the very message about faith that we preach: If you openly declare
that Jesus is Lord and believe in your heart that God
raised him from the dead, you will be saved. For it is
by believing in your heart that you are made right with
God, and it is by openly declaring your faith that you
are saved (Romans 10:8-10, New Living Translation).

When we come to the realization that we are in need of a
Savior, we *breathe* in the revelation of Jesus Christ, sent from
heaven, born of a virgin, crucified, and resurrected to forgive us
of all sin and iniquity so we can be sons and daughters of God
once again! We breathe in the life of Christ, anointed and appointed to return the authority we lost in separation from God

the Father, so we can represent Him on this earth now and for all eternity. We are alive as Christ is alive! And as long as we *breathe again*, we sustain that life in Him. We were never meant to take that first and only breath. The first breath, though essential to this Christian experience, cannot be the only breath. We cannot reserve that first breath for later. If we want to experience the fullness of God, we must use it. Some of us manage our lives like we fill our gas tanks, fill it up and wait till it empties out at the end of the week, trying to preserve it or get the last little drip out. I tend to forget to put gas in my car and then find myself praying, "Lord, please get me to the gas station before I run out. Thank you, faithful Father!" Fortunately, my prayers have worked every time. But what we cannot afford to do is wait till we're out of breath spiritually expecting to be full of the Holy Spirit. We must have another encounter with Him.

The Word of God so powerfully explains that we "overcome by the blood of the Lamb and the word of our testimony" (Revelation 12:11 NKJV). With this weapon, we remind ourselves and the devil, our arch enemy, that we had an experience, but we cannot limit our spirituality with the One Who gives us life to just one encounter or experience. We must say, "Breath of God, fill me once again!"

I remember my first significant encounter with God. I had grown up in the church, attending almost every day of the week with my family for prayer meetings, Bible studies, food preparations, Sunday school, midday service, and night ser-vices, revivals, and even foot washings! I knew a lot of scripture, but I didn't know Jesus, the Savior of my soul. And although I had some great experiences with the Lord growing up, I didn't understand that I was saved by His grace and not by my works. With this lack of revelation, I couldn't save myself enough to allow God to save me. In my senior year of college, and many painful experiences later, I encountered the only One who saves, Jesus Christ! I will never forget this most important encounter with my Lord; He took the broken pieces of my life, healed me, delivered me from myself, and gave me a brand-new life! That was undoubtedly the first real breath or infilling I re-ceived of the Holy Spirit. I was completely transformed! This encounter led to more encounters and a greater desire for more of Him. You will know you have had an encounter with God if you have an insatiable desire for more. No matter how much of Him you have, you will always have room for more. He's too big! He's too creative! He's too dynamic and awesome! There will always be another breath to be had. So I challenge you thus far, breathe again. Stop holding your breath in life and just breathe again!

Chapter Two

Recognizing Who God Is

"Let the heavens rejoice, and let the earth be glad; Let the sea roar, and all its fullness; Let the field be joyful, and all that is in it. Then all the trees of the woods will rejoice before the Lord" (Psalms 96:11-12 New King James Version).

"This is the day the Lord has made; We will rejoice and be glad in it" Psalms 118:24 (NKJV).

> *It is good to give thanks to the Lord, to sing praises to the Most High. It is good to proclaim your unfailing love in the morning, your faithfulness in the evening.*
> *Psalms 92:1-2 NKJV*

Every day, all of creation rejoices and recognizes who God is whether people recognize Him or not. At every turn, His handiwork speaks and communicates to all things living that He is God. When we, as His children, go a step further to declare all He's done and who He is, the miraculous happens. Everything around us comes to attention at the sound of praise to the King of Kings! The Psalms is such an incredible book loaded with praise and worship to the Lord that you can't help but rejoice when you read the chapters exalting and adoring God. What does rejoice mean? Have joy again! Read some of David's Psalms right now and experience the joy that fills your heart!

There are too many to name. Even in the times when David was in the throes of despair, he could not help but turn his mind to praise his God. Why? God is undeniable. He is the lifter of our head, the One who gives grace and mercy beyond measure. His ways are unfathomable - we cannot begin to understand or conceive His glorious nature, a nature He makes available to us every time we breathe!

Whenever we don't take the time to *breathe* Him in and praise, we rob ourselves of the opportunity to connect with God and recognize who He is and all He's done for us.

"Enter His gates with thanksgiving and into His courts with praise. Be thankful to Him and bless His name" (Psalm 100:4 New King James Version (NKJV).

It is very difficult to be overcome by stress and anxiety when you begin to praise God. Praise gets everything out of the way, so heaven opens. The devil can't stand praise. He cannot compete with the awesome power of the Almighty God! He just can't. His smokescreen dissipates when we praise - judgment is executed upon him and he can find no solace or rock to hide behind. He simply runs away. That is why deliverance lies in the wake of praise; we recognize God's power through praise, and the enemy of our souls is cast out of our lives. It's like fire upon his feet. He cannot stand and pursue. He is put to shame when we praise.

However, you cannot truly praise God until repentance takes place. Repentance is a change of heart and mind. When you repent, you are deciding to abandon your previous mindset or way of thinking and living and turn to God in humility. This active step gives you the freedom to praise Him because He is God - He forgives and makes you brand new! No more chains! No muzzle! No shame, no guilt, or condemnation! Don't let pride strangle your freedom and choke your peace and joy. Life - a full blessed life belongs to you.

Psalms 34: 1-7 says:

> I will bless the Lord at all times; His praise shall continually be in my mouth. My soul shall make its boast in the Lord; The humble shall hear of it and be glad. Oh, magnify the Lord with me, and let us exalt His name together. I sought the Lord, and He heard me, and delivered me from all my fears. They looked to Him and were radiant, and their faces were not ashamed. This poor man cried out, and the Lord heard him, and saved him out of all his troubles. The angel of the Lord encamps all around those who fear Him and delivers them (NKJV).

Praise is active, and it activates supernatural movement in several ways:

1. It recognizes the Almighty, Omnipotent, Omnipresent God.

When God is praised, His nature and presence expand in our lives. In all His power and might, He "becomes" a personal God. Not only is God everywhere, but He is right where we are.

2. It gets the Father's attention.

"Sing to God, you kingdoms of the earth; Oh, sing praises to the Lord...Indeed, He sends out His voice, a mighty voice" (Psalms 68:32-33). In having the Father's attention, we know He hears and responds to us. In praise, He sends a mighty voice that compels the atmosphere to obey, and at the same time, He listens. God is the most avid listener and yet the most effective counselor. He knows and understands the details and the things we don't have words to express. He literally inhabits our praises!

3. It releases angelic armies.

Heaven and earth respond to the Word of God being spoken or released from individuals. "For the kingdom of God is not in word but in power" (I Corinthians 4:20, NKJV). The angels give power or credence to the authority and will of God. They assemble to serve God and those who represent Him.

4. It ignites a fire and passion for the Holy Spirit to manifest Himself.

Active praise wakes up your sleepy soul to allow the fresh breath of the Holy Spirit to invade you and ignite a fire that only He can give. Holy Spirit inspires and empowers you to do what you wouldn't ordinarily do. He is not toxic like the vices of this world; He is liberating. He gives you boldness and passion to express His nature. Holy Spirit is your superpower!

5. It makes Satan tremble and run.

Your praise is an obnoxious clanging cymbal in the ear of Satan! When you praise the King of Kings for who He is and all He has done for you, it is as if the devil's skin begins to crawl with thousands of mosquitoes, sucking the life right out of him. He becomes incapacitated to overcome you! The Bible tells us that he trembles and is afraid at the sound of the Word of God. This is a good time to stop and punish the devil for trying your life!

6. *It invades darkness.*

Praise says, "God, You are great! There is nothing impossible to You. You are the God of all creation. Be lifted up - You are Lord, and You are the ultimate victor over every enemy that could ever be named!" Now that you've had a few moments to meditate on praise, do you feel the light of the glory of God where you are? Darkness must immediately leave. Whenever the name of the Lord is lifted up, light is evident, and the darkness cannot withstand it. Just turn on a light in a dark room and simply see what transpires! It's that simple.

7. *It breaks strongholds, mindsets, and chains of sin.*

Your praise to God recognizes His power and dominion and releases a consuming fire that breaks down strongholds, mindsets, and the chains associated with them. How? Because God is almighty and all-powerful, true praise opens Heaven's gates and changes everything it touches. The Holy Spirit immediately moves into your atmosphere and begins to transform it in accordance with Heaven's atmosphere.

Take a few minutes right now and allow your praise to God to transform your atmosphere - bring the kingdom of Heaven down to earth. Take that praise break - Take a *breath* of the power of God and be a witness and testimony of His greatness!

Chapter Three

Expression of Intimacy

David, God's handpicked "son," chosen and appointed to be king over Israel - actually, earmarked to be the greatest king of Israel - was tested, tormented, and exhausted for the first part of his adulthood, running from his enemies and King Saul, the current king of Israel. Throughout the Psalms, David worshiped God and cried out to God to save him, celebrated the victories he had along the way, and then worshipped again! He said:

The Lord is my light and my salvation; Whom shall I fear? The Lord is the strength of my life; Of whom shall I be afraid? When the wicked came against me to eat up my flesh, My enemies and foes, They stumbled and fell. Though an army may encamp against me, my heart shall not fear; Though war may rise against me, in this I will be confident. One thing I have desired of the Lord, that will I seek: That I may dwell in the house of the Lord all the days of my life, to behold the beauty of the Lord, and to inquire in His temple. For in the time of trouble He shall hide me in His pavilion; In the secret place of His tabernacle He shall hide me; He shall set me high upon a rock (Psalms 27:1-5 NKJV).

We can see from this passage of scripture that David learned to depend upon God; some days may have been easier than others. Had he not, the calamity he faced daily would have suffocated David and disrupted the plan of God for his life. David was intertwined with the Almighty God, the One Who is holy and full of love and compassion. There is no end to His faithfulness and mercy. David learned how to trust God on the mountain, in the valley, in the cave, in the light, and in the darkness. He had to keep breathing God in and accessing the tangibility of their relationship in order to continue on and stay alive.

What are you holding onto that you refuse to put in the hands of God? What has you holding your breath wondering if things will turn out right? Worship brings you into the courts of the

King, where there is open communication, safety, peace, and joy. There is no other place in the heavens or earth that can translate you into a holy and pure realm outside of your own capacity that totally transforms your very nature. Worship is the key that opens this door to the Heavenly Father. He loves to be "Daddy"! He loves to be wanted, needed, and enjoyed. "In Your presence is fullness of joy; At Your right hand are pleasures forevermore" (Psalm 16:11). Forever is an unimaginable amount of time and yet He reserves this privilege for His children!

Throughout the scriptures, David is known by God as a "man after God's heart." **David actively sought the heart of God. Therefore, he had the heart of God.** There is no other way to commune with Him but through worship. There is no way to touch Him and be touched by Him but through worship. There is no shortcut.

Whenever you breathe worship unto the Lord, you set yourself up for a supernatural encounter with Him. He responds to a heart that seeks Him and rewards such with His tangible presence. In this kingdom reality, He is our Creator and Lord, God Almighty Who is all-powerful and all-sufficient. He sustains us. He is everlasting and enduring, our banner, our peace, and our provider. He is our Healer and the Lord who sends His angels out to be a help. God is always there.

He is everything. The I Am. He is not the I Was, or I Will Be, but the I Am, always Present. So whatever need we find ourselves facing, He Is - He is right in the middle of that need - if we choose Him to be.

We've talked about being born again as your first breath, but continuing to breathe is the work of the Holy Spirit, being filled with the Holy Spirit over and over again. Through this infilling, God reveals His mysteries. The Holy Spirit "searches all things, even the deep things of God" (I Corinthians 1:10). Why is this important and necessary? When life throws curveballs at you, you need something, or rather someone, supernatural to step in and reveal the mysteries needed to bring the correct perspective into your situation. You need power to overcome.

How does this work? ***While praise opens the gates of Heaven, worship takes you to the throne room.*** It is the difference in knowing what God can do and knowing Him.

As a deceived believer, I could praise Him because I believed in God, but without a personal relationship with Him, I could not begin to understand the depths of God.

It is in His presence that everything comes into focus and the correct perspective is realized because God becomes greater, mightier, more accessible, and alive in your life, even in the situations that have you holding your breath. The Bible says to "taste and see that the Lord is good" (Psalm 34:8 NKJV). There is an action that needs to be done on your part - taste. God's part is to be good.

In thinking about the story of Naomi and Ruth and all that they had lost only to gain the favor and mercy of the Lord,

I am reminded of how God interacts with us. Elimelech, Naomi's husband moved away from their land and residence because of a famine. He thought he would be better off in a different place, with a different people who did not believe in Jehovah God. The Bible tells us that his sons found wives from the country of Moab, a place that served other gods. They had been blessed in their land of Bethlehem, Judah, surrounded by their family and friends. When they found themselves in the middle of a famine, Elimelech thought it best to leave. Had he followed God's plan of provision, he would have found help in the time of his need in the land God placed him in. Understanding that there are times when the Lord moves us, we must be sensitive to the Holy Spirit for direction and timing. He moved his family there temporarily, but the scriptures then tell us that he decided to stay there. Afterwards, Elimelech died. Then his sons married outside of their faith, and they, too, died. Naomi, whose name means pleasant, was left alone with two daughters-in-law. Ruth 1:6 says that Naomi heard it was well in Judah, so it was good to return. Whenever we step out of the will of God or find ourselves in disobedience to the will of God, we open doors God never intended to be open. Naomi told her daughters-in-law to return to their home, the house of their mother, and their gods. With a sad heart, Orpah said her goodbyes, but Ruth vowed to never leave Naomi. She said, "For wherever you go, I will go; And wherever you lodge, I will lodge; your people will be my people, And your God, my God. Where you die, I will die, and there will be buried. The Lord do so to me, and more also, if anything by death parts you and me" (Ruth 1:16-17 NKJV).

That had to be a tremendous sacrifice and commitment on Ruth's part that, is rarely, if ever, seen. Let's mull this over a bit. Orpah leaves with a heavy heart, likely full of disappointment, regret, and pain, while Ruth, though probably encumbered by life's disappointments, chooses the way of progress and hope. We don't hear anything else about Oprah, but Ruth's story does not end. She goes down in history as an important, faithful descendant of Jesus Christ! Her end was much greater than her beginning. Ruth chose not to run and hide but to live and serve. She stood by her commitment to her mother-in-law and her God.

Chapter Four

Relationship Goals

To be intimate with Jesus is the most precious place, the most precious position to be in because He is always safe. There is no safer place to be than in the arms of the Savior! No matter how young, how old, how wealthy, or poor; how much you've done, good and bad, He is the safe place. In His presence is the only place that leaves you full and not empty and unsatisfied. Our closest human confidant is a blessing from God, but even he or she cannot satisfy the longing we all have to be complete and completely free. Only Jesus can stand in that place of perfect goodness! He is completely lovable and completely trustworthy. There are times when you don't understand how God is working and how He is moving, but intimacy can only be accessed where there is trust.

Ask yourself the question, who do you trust and why? What makes that person so remarkable that you give yourself to them unabashedly? It takes faith to trust people. For some it is easier to trust than others because of experiences that color our judgment and cloud our hearts. But trust begins with a decision that says yes, I will. After this decision is made, trust is built and grows over the expanse of that relationship. When our hearts are broken, trust can be shattered and sometimes never regained, unless we choose to walk in forgiveness. We often must decide to forgive and rebuild the trust that was lost in those cases. God forgives us all day long, no matter the mistake, and still makes Himself available. He never withholds His love from us. The Bible directs us to always trust God because there is blessing, mercy, grace, and safety in doing so.

Now, what makes Him trust us? The Bible says in James:

My brethren, count it all joy when you fall into various trials, knowing that the testing of your faith produces patience. But let patience have *its* perfect work, that you may be perfect and complete, lacking nothing… Blessed *is* the man who endures temptation; for when he has been approved, he will receive the crown of life which the Lord has promised to those who love Him (James 1:2-4, 12 NKJV).

Yes, we are tested and allowed to go through many trials

in our lives, but if we endure, we will see the fruit or growth of our perseverance. God can trust us when we receive His instructions and obey Him. He doesn't expect us to be perfect, but He does expect us to listen to His voice and follow Him. Like a loving parent with his son or daughter, he corrects us and disciplines us so that we learn and grow. Though it can be painful in the moment, it is necessary and beneficial *(See Hebrews 12:5-11)*.

Therefore, God trusts us when we follow Him with our whole heart. He is quick to show us what we can have and what we can achieve in life, but we must have the character to sustain those blessings. God is not wasteful. He does things on purpose. He gave His very best, Jesus Christ, His only son, to live a sinless, thankless life, so that we would have an example to follow. Then led him to be slaughtered at the hand of his enemies so that we would be free from sin and death, healed and delivered, with the incredible opportunity to live forever in paradise with Him! Those are authentic relationship goals - to give His life, a ransom for many (See Matthew 20:28). No relationship can withstand selfishness, so God is not selfish, whereas we are. He trusts us according to our lack of selfishness because no relationship can survive and thrive if it is one-sided. Trust God - He is worth it. His love is worth it. His peace is worth it. His joy is worth it. He is perfect in all His ways, therefore worthy of our trust.

God sees us as we are meant to be but picks us up where we are and says, "Breathe; take a breath and trust me with you."

"Our confidence is in Jesus Christ in whom we have boldness and confident access through faith in Him [that is, our faith gives us sufficient courage to freely and openly approach God through Christ]" (Ephesians 3:12 AMP). If you continue reading the rest of this chapter in Ephesians, your heart will expand with the revelation that God deeply loves us and makes Himself completely available to us! We can be confident in this one thing - He moved heaven and earth to have a lasting relationship with us. It really is incomprehensible, but so real!

How do we develop this intimate relationship with

Christ? Within the heart of the Creator and the destiny of His creation lies the perfect love story - the epitome of the greatest romance ever to be told, ever to be written, ever to be shown. "My beloved is mine, and I am his" (Song of Solomon 2:16). I just cannot resist a good romance. I enjoy the suspense, the "chase," the vulnerability, the getting to know each other, and ultimately, when the man and woman pledge their love to each other. Every love story has opposition of sorts, whether it's internal or external, which adds to the suspense of wondering if it's the real thing and worth being selfless for. King Solomon had 700 wives plus extras! That's a whole lot of romance and potentially, a lot of conflict.

First, we spend time with Him, meditating on Him and His word. In the Gospels, Jesus speaks about the kingdom of God to all the people in parables or pictures, but only reveals the mysteries of the parables to his disciples, those closest to Him. They were hungry, as evident by them following Him, and their hearts were open to understand. Many times, the disciples had questions and didn't understand everything Jesus shared with them, but they stuck with Him and allowed themselves to see Jesus and be taught by Him.

Throughout Jesus' ministry in the New Testament, He instructed people to follow Him. Simply, follow Him. I believe that is a main key in remaining faithful in your relationship with God. We must follow Him wherever He chooses. Yes, that is going to take a lot of trust!

Final exams were upon me and I had been up late studying, writing papers, preparing projects in my senior year of college. I remember feeling so exhausted and as I lay my head down to sleep for a few hours, I began thanking God for saving me, for loving me and I drifted off to sleep, I asked Him to please wake me up. (I'm a hard sleeper, or at least I used to be, so an alarm was merely a dream interrupter for me.) At that moment, I had complete confidence that Jesus would indeed wake me up. Several hours later, I was awakened by a voice; it was audible - "Kiya, wake up." I immediately was wide awake! At that point in my spiritual life, I would have never imagined hearing the Lord's voice, literally!

People didn't believe me - I've told this story many times, and I still get that look of "yeah, right!" But I tell you, 26 years later, the thought of Jesus calling my name for something seemingly minor and probably unnecessary, was life-changing and to this day fills me with that warm, satisfying, yet insatiable feeling of being loved, knowing without a doubt, He loves ME! HE - the God of the whole universe, in the heavens and in the earth, LOVES me. I've often asked why He chose to speak to me that day in such a personal way. He always responds with, "Because I love you and I need you to know that. I need you to know that you're important and your love and your life is special to me." Wow - as I write this, I feel his overwhelming presence - My Beloved is mine and I am His. It's that simple, but so deep, so sweet, and intimate. It has never mattered to me that people, some of my closest friends, didn't believe me when I've relayed this story to them. What has always mattered is that from that day forward, my heart was captured by the most amazing person in the entire world. Jesus. He never leaves. He's always available. He doesn't disappear with the wind - He's always the same, yet He expresses Himself in ways that surprises and confounds me. His love never changes - it still draws me and woos me closer and closer to Him. He knows how to put the dreaminess in my eyes. He knows how to capture my heart when I get distracted and busy with life. Jesus knows what I think, how I think, how I feel, when I'm sad or disappointed, when I'm excited or expectant. Whatever it is I am missing in my life; He fills it. I was laboring over how to begin this chapter of relation-ship goals and asked Him to show me what needs to be said and He so aptly reminded me of His love. He has shown His love for me in so many amazing ways over the years, from the small-est of things to His giving me a beautiful family whom I adore, but it has all stemmed from this most personal experience of something He really didn't have to do, but He did.

We cannot begin to really love another until we experience the unconditional love of God - He is love. He exudes love. He breathes love. It's almost unexplainable, but in trying to, look at the Song of Solomon and see how much He dotes on and adores His bride. It's a perfect picture of how much the Bridegroom thinks of His Bride and how enraptured they are with each the other. In these passages God is revealing how intimate this relationship is supposed to be. The Bridegroom calls out to the Bride, searches for and longs for her. And she, in return, meditates on how amazing he is, how beautiful he is, and how she lives to please him. She can't help but tell all her friends about him - he is that magnanimous! She tells them in chapter 2 of Song of Solomon:

He brought me to the banqueting house, and his banner over me *was* love. Sustain me with cakes of raisins, Refresh me with apples, for I *am* lovesick. His left hand *is* under my head, and his right hand embraces me. I charge you, O daughters of Jerusalem, by the gazelles or by the does of the field, do not stir up nor awaken love until it pleases (2:4-7).

She basically warns them not to awaken love until you're ready, because it will consume you and overtake you in the most pleasant of ways! We can look at this scripture naturally and see the implication of not to stir or awaken love in our lives until we are prepared and certain of who God has chosen for us because it could be to our detriment to do so. To all the men and women out there who have had their hearts broken, can I get an Amen?

The Shulamite woman doesn't express this sentiment with disappointment or regret. On the contrary, she shares her Beloved's heart toward her and the requests he asks of her with pride and admiration. She is in love.

Those are relationship goals - the love of the Bridegroom toward the Bride and her devotion to him. If we loved our spouses like the "couple" depicted in these verses, there would be many more marriages that last till death do they part instead of the staggering statistics of our time.

She cannot help but testify of the love she has found and how wonderful her Bridegroom is. You know, the more we praise and worship the Lord, the more He reveals of Himself and demonstrates who He is. Mountains and obstacles crumble before His presence, at the sound of voice. When He is near, the sun shines brighter, the stars twinkle just for you, and your world is in order even if they appear to not be. Again, it's almost incomprehensible! I am struck by the depiction of the Bride-groom seeing his Bride in chapter 4 of the Message Bible.

You're so beautiful, my darling, so beautiful, and your dove eyes are veiled by your hair as it flows and shimmers, like a flock of goats in the distance streaming down a hillside in the sunshine. Your smile is generous and full— expressive and strong and clean. Your lips are jewel red, your mouth elegant and inviting, your veiled cheeks soft and radiant. The smooth, lithe lines of your neck command notice—all heads turn in awe and admiration! Your breasts are like fawns, twins of a gazelle, grazing among the first spring flowers. The sweet, fragrant curves of your body, the soft, spiced contours of your flesh. Invite me, and I come. I stay until dawn breathes its light and nightslips away. You're beautiful from head to toe, my dear love, beautiful beyond compare, absolutely flawless. Come with me from Lebanon, my bride. Leave Lebanon behind, and come. Leave your high mountain hideaway. Abandon your wilderness seclusion, where you keep company with lions and panthers guard your safety. You've captured my heart, dear friend. You looked at me, and I fell in love. One look my way and I was hopelessly in love! How beautiful your love, dear, dear friend— far more pleasing than a fine, rare wine, your fragrance more exotic than select spices (Song of Solomon 4:1-15 Message Bible).

What a beautiful love story - a romance of all romances! This is what God thinks about us - His creation. Admiring His own work, He sets us up to give Him the glory, praise, and honor we were created to express to Him. It amazes me that no two of mankind are exactly alike, which means when we express our desire and love for God, He hears and sees the beauty and authenticity of Himself in us. He is love, but we become love as we adore Him. That's intoxicating! "How precious are his thoughts toward us…Great is the sum of them" (Psalm 139:17). In Him we move and live and have our being. We cannot exist outside of Him. That's why when we are not connected to God, we are missing something. We could have everything on this earth available and still be unhappy and unfulfilled. We all have a measure of God, a measure of faith, by way of the very breath we breathe. However, we need the love of God, personally. When we have it and He has us, there's no turning back - He satisfies!

Chapter Five

The Challenge

Many times, we find being satisfied a challenge because we tend to want the immediate reward, the immediate gratification. Haven't you heard the adage - "Good things come to those who wait"? That is partly true - We learn, grow, and mature in accordance with our level of patience. In the same way that we don't choose a mate overnight to spend the rest of our lives with, God doesn't give us the "Lamborghini" of life at 16 when we've just gotten our license. For most things, there is a process that must take place for us to develop understanding and wisdom as we mature as Christians, appreciating who God is, what He does, and how He operates in and through us. I used to sing an old song by the great gospel singer, Andraé Crouch, "Through It All". In one verse of this song it says, "For if I'd never have a problem, I wouldn't know that God could solve them; I'd never know what faith in God could do." This portion of the verse is so true because we cannot understand a need for a savior unless we experience the need for rescuing. In other words, we learn to turn to God for anything and everything because we know, through experience, that He will rescue and save us every time. Going back to the Shulamite woman in the Song of Solomon, we are reminded to not awaken love until we're ready because once it's awake, we are captured by the sweetness of its nectar, a very good thing as long as you have connected with the right person. So, the key in this relationship is to love and be loved wholeheartedly while enjoying the journey of learning, loving, and developing in the arms of the Bridegroom.

Chapter Six

Learning to Breathe

I've often thought that rhythm is something you must be born with. Either it is inherent in you or it isn't. The churches I have always been a part of or around have been multicultural and so as you can imagine, we've always had lots of fun laughing at people praising and dancing to different beats, some even in the same family, like mine. Some of us can dance, some of us can clap, and some of us just move to the rhythm in our heads! I'm kind of in the middle. But since I am also somewhat of a spaz, that varies. My husband tells me he's "more ethnic" than I am, (in some cases,) maybe, but not rhythm. Now that's not to say I've got the beat down all the time; sometimes I follow the beat, and other times, the beat has to follow me! At least that is what I discuss with my metronome as I clunk out a worship tune on the keyboard. Throughout my "dancing career," I've realized that rhythm can be learned if you want it badly enough. It takes patience and persistence. You can't give up. I remember in college, over a couple decades ago when music was cool and clean, that my friends would laugh hysterically at my dance moves (kind of like my kids do now), trying to teach me how not to look like I was hurting myself. It was atrocious! But I love music and I love to move, so I kept at it, until they weren't laughing anymore. I had somewhat arrived. It took time, but once I got it, I was always dancing! (Today, the dance moves are a little out of my league, so I just go with the flow – at church!

Learning to *breathe* with God takes patience and persistence. You can't give up. At first, it's easy. Why? Because you make the decision to follow Christ and you come out of the dark cave you have been dwelling in, and suddenly, you can see the Light. It's miraculous - The sun is brighter, people are more beautiful, your kids are amazing, your dog is patient and happy, your cat is friendly. Even your fish are swimming to their special tune! Everything is magnified in all its glory...until the bottom falls out and life happens. A hiccup in your day can turn into the tragedy of the week and you need to know how to take the next breath. God is so good, naturally, that He knows what we can handle and when we can handle it. So, He covers us, fills us to overflowing, heals and makes us whole so we can taste and see His goodness. But as a Father, He also teaches us and with any subject in a classroom, there will be tests to determine mastery. The longer you walk with the Lord, the more He will teach you to trust Him and trust Him in everything. That requires taking a deep breath of the Holy Spirit every chance you get. He is faithful to fill and satisfy, but He won't force Himself on you, ever. The Holy Spirit is gentle, easy to entreat, and He needs to be welcomed. He doesn't respond to your frustration but responds to your faith in the Father to handle everything you face in life and lead you in the right direction. We tend to stop "breathing" or depending on God when we think we've got life all figured out. Sometimes, God allows us to get to the point of extreme frustration or allows challenges to come so that we need to look to Him, to seek Him. Remember the Shulamite woman? She was either looking for her Beloved, seeking him out, or following Him and every word he uttered. If we behaved the same towards our Lord, we would see more of His presence and less of ourselves and our problems.

Learning to breathe is just that - learning. It is a process that we must embrace. If we allow our relationship to grow cold, that will lead us to abandon God altogether. He is always moving and doing something amazing, wanting to reveal Himself more and more to us, but we cannot abandon Him in the learning process. His desire is for us to move from glory to glory and faith to faith. As we breathe Him in, we grow, mature, and fall completely in love with God so much so that we are one with Him. Jesus prayed that we would be one in Him even as he was one in the Father (John 17:20-22). In this unity, we develop a rhythm with God. For example, marriage between a man and a woman can only withstand the test of time with true commitment to one another along with the understanding that as they mature, their relationship should mature; therefore, every area of growth and change must be accepted by both husband and wife. Now, if one spouse changes negatively because of bad experiences, they both have a decision to make; do they continue to support their spouse and help get them to a better place, or do they abandon ship? Does the hurting spouse accept that they need help, or do they drive their spouse away? One person alone cannot make or break a marriage, even though one spouse may have committed the worse sin imagined. In a marriage, if you withhold parts of yourself from your spouse, it will be a dysfunctional relationship. You may be able to commit for the long haul, but you won't be completely free to enjoy all the benefits that should be present in a marriage. Being one with God works in the same way. He promises to never leave us or forsake us, no matter what, but we have a responsibility to keep our end of the bargain and give ourselves to Him completely.

Intimacy with God is a learning and growing process. He loves us completely and unconditionally – therefore, we can trust His commitment to us. However, when we stop nurturing our connection with God, it forces Him to step back and allow us to "live" without Him, without His instruction and wisdom.

In understanding the marriage relationship, there must be continual intimacy - you must keep breathing the very nature of God so that [His] "joy remains in you and your joy remain full" (John 15:11).

Yes, this is possible. He is the air we breathe! Therefore, in this recognition of God as our life source, the breath we inhale every day, there is an exchange of life for life; His life for our life. It is impossible for us to control whether we breathe or not. That's not our decision, whether you believe in Christ or not. Even when one takes their own life, it is God who allows that person to live or die.

Breathe while you can breathe and inhale the goodness and sweetness of the Holy Spirit, who teaches us and leads us in all things. The scriptures tell us to call upon the breath of God for life as in Job 33:4; "The Spirit of God has made me, And the breath of the Almighty gives me life". Every single situation and challenge we come up against must bow down to the name that is greater than any name, Yahweh - I AM, the

Lord God Almighty, who was and is and is to come. Everything created in the heavens and in the earth must submit its existence to the will of God. Nothing exists outside of Him, so when we refresh our breath with the One who created us, we are revived again and again. The same surrender it took to accept Jesus Christ as our Savior is the same principle and instruction we must follow to continue a vibrant and fresh relationship with Him. Living life in this world, with all its imperfections is surely enough to stifle the air we breathe, suffocating us, but in Romans 8:31-39, Paul clearly puts a life with Christ in perspective when he declares:

What should we say then? Since God is on our side, who can be against us? God did not spare his own Son. He gave him up for us all. Then won't he also freely give us everything else? Who can bring any charge against God's chosen ones? God makes us right with himself. Then who can sentence us to death? No one. Christ Jesus is at the right hand of God and is also praying for us. He died. More than that, he was raised to life. Who can separate us from Christ's love? Can trouble or hard times or harm or hunger? Can nakedness or danger or war? It is written, Because of you, we face death all day long. We are considered as sheep to be killed. No! In all these things we are more than winners! We owe it all to Christ, who has loved us. I am absolutely sure that not even death or life can separate us from God's love. Not even angels or demons, the present or the future, or any powers can separate us. Not even the highest places or the lowest, or anything else in all creation can separate us. Nothing at all can ever separate us from God's love. That's because of what Christ Jesus our Lord has done (New International Reader's Version – NIRV).

Christ gives us the opportunity to be like Him - He is the Door we walk through where there is victory and ultimate freedom. In Him we experience the life He designed for us to live. We learn to breathe with the very breath of God that created, transformed, and sustains us each and every day. Now, those are relationship goals!

Appendix

Chapter 2: Additional Scripture References taken from The Holy Bible, New King James Version.

1. **Recognizes the Almighty:**

   Habakkuk 3:3-6, Psalm 91,

   Psalm 77:12-4, Psalm 29:4, Psalm 95,

   Psalm 150

2. **Gets the Father's Attention:**

   Psalm 24:7-10, Psalm 18:46-50,

   Psalm 55:16

3. **Releases Angelic Hosts:**

   Psalm 46:11,

   Psalm 91:11, Psalm 103:20-21

4. **Ignites a Fire and Passion:**

   Psalm 97:3-6

5. **Makes Satan Tremble and Run:**

   Psalm18:3, James 2:19, Matthew 4:11,

   Matthew 16:18, Psalm 144:1,

   Ephesians 6:11

6. **Invades Darkness:**

   Ephesians 6:12, Matthew 8:28-29,

   Psalm 36:9, John 1:5,

   Ephesians 5:8,13-14, Matthew 5:15-16,

   Psalm 89:15

7. **Breaks Strongholds, Mindsets, and Chains of Sin:**

   John 12:35, I John 1:7,

   Isaiah 60

About the Author

Kiya Cordeau, co-founder of David Cordeau Ministry, Inc., is an ordained pastor who ministers the transforming Gospel with simplicity and humor to release a prophetic word to the whole family. She leads in spiritual warfare, intercession, and prophetic worship, empowering people to live victorious lives and expand the Kingdom of God. Kiya is available for conferences and retreats, including marriage workshops. Her career training is in secondary education; she has taught and served in the public and private sectors and currently teaches high school in Broward County, FL. Kiya and her husband, David have been married for 26 years and have three amazing children: Elisha, Cherie, and Jordan.

www.ingramcontent.com/pod-product-compliance
Lightning Source LLC
LaVergne TN
LVHW051200080426
835508LV00021B/2725